THE BRITISH COLONIES IN NORTH AMERICA

BY PETER BENOIT

CHILDREN'S PRESS®
An Imprint of Scholastic Inc.
New York Toronto London Auckland Sydney
Mexico City New Delhi Hong Kong
Danbury, Connecticut

BRINGING HISTORY to LIFE

Content Consultant
James Marten, PhD
Professor and Chair, History Department
Marquette University
Milwaukee, Wisconsin

Library of Congress Cataloging-in-Publication Data

Benoit, Peter, 1955–
  The British colonies in North America / by Peter Benoit.
      p. cm.—(Cornerstones of freedom)
  Includes bibliographical references and index.
  ISBN 978-0-531-23602-4 (library binding) — ISBN 978-0-531-21960-7 (pbk.)
  1. United States—History—Colonial period, ca. 1600–1775—Juvenile
literature. I. Title.
  E188.B46 2013
  973.2—dc23   2012030353

Photographs © 2013: age fotostock/Fotosearch RM: cover; AP Images:
38 (Bruce Smith), 5 bottom, 5 top, 7, 17, 20, 25, 27, 32, 36, 37, 41, 42, 44, 47,
49, 57 top (North Wind Picture Archives); Bridgeman Art Library/Currier
& Ives/Yale University Art Gallery, New Haven, CT: 15; iStockphoto/trav-
eler1116: 4 bottom, 48; Library of Congress/William Sartain: 51; Media
Bakery/Krista Rossow: back cover; National Archives and Records
Administration: 54; National Park Service/Colonial National Historical Park:
4 top, 13; North Wind Picture Archives: 14, 24; Superstock, Inc.: 10 (Stock
Montage), 2, 3, 46; The Granger Collection: 50 (Charles Willson Peale),
40 (Edwin James Meeker), 30 (Gauthier and Faden), 23 (Howard Pyle), 8
(John Bettes the Younger), 45 (Junius Brutus Stearns), 11, 12, 18, 22, 26,
28, 29, 31, 35, 39, 55, 57 bottom; The Image Works: 6 (BeBa/Iberfoto), 21, 56
(Print Collector/HIP).

Maps by XNR Productions, Inc.

Did you know that studying history can be fun?

BRING HISTORY TO LIFE by becoming a history investigator. Examine the evidence (primary and secondary source materials); cross-examine the people and witnesses. Take a look at what was happening at the time—but be careful! What happened years ago might suddenly become incredibly interesting and change the way you think!

Contents

The Colonization of America

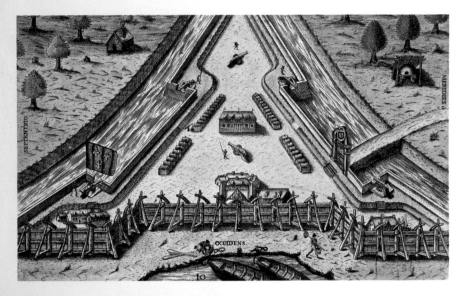

French settlers built Fort Caroline along the St. John's River.

The Europeans who came to the present-day United States were determined to establish colonies that lasted. But it wasn't easy. It began with a series of failures and brief successes. In 1564, the French established a colony at Fort Caroline, in what is now Jacksonville, Florida. The next year, Spain set up an important settlement at

ST. AUGUSTINE, FLORIDA, IS THE

St. Augustine, on Florida's northeastern coast. Within months of St. Augustine's founding, the Spanish launched an attack on Fort Caroline and captured it.

England's early attempts at American colonization also met with failure. But it eventually did succeed in establishing 13 thriving colonies. Creating successful settlements was a challenge. Early settlers struggled against disease, weather, and unwelcoming Native Americans. Tensions and conflict often arose among the colonies as they developed along different social, **economic**, and political lines.

Despite their differences, the English colonists in America eventually found common ground. They joined together and threw off British rule. American history is largely defined by the struggles of the early colonists. These struggles continue to ripple through American life.

Today, the St. Augustine colony lives on as a city in Florida.

OLDEST CITY IN THE UNITED STATES.

CHAPTER 1

IN THE BEGINNING

Queen Elizabeth I hoped to gain wealth for England by establishing colonies in America.

In 1584, England's Queen

Elizabeth I granted the explorer Sir Walter Raleigh a charter to establish a colony in North America. Spanish and Portuguese explorers had begun exporting silver and gold from North and South America to their mother countries decades earlier. Spain had grown wealthy, and its powerful naval fleet posed a threat to England. Elizabeth hoped to use gold discovered in America to improve England's navy.

Sir Walter Raleigh hoped to start a colony on Roanoke Island, in present-day North Carolina.

The Failure of Roanoke

Raleigh's first expedition landed on the coast of what is now North Carolina on July 4, 1584. A more substantial expedition, led by Richard Grenville, departed Plymouth, England, the following April. Grenville and his crew explored the coastline and the Native American settlements in that area. During their visit, the explorers accused the Aquascogoc people of stealing a silver cup. As revenge, they burned down the Aquascogoc village. This would come back to haunt the explorers.

Shortly after, Grenville left to establish a colony with 107 men on nearby Roanoke Island. Grenville soon left for England to bring back more men and fresh supplies, promising to return the following April.

By April 1586, Grenville's relief fleet had not returned. The colonists were dangerously low on supplies. Then the Aquascogoc launched an attack on the colony in retaliation for the burning of their village. The settlers beat back the attack, but they no longer wanted any part of settling America. Soon after, English **privateer** Francis Drake docked at Roanoke following his own raids on Spanish treasure ships in the Caribbean Sea. Drake offered to bring the colonists back to England. They gladly accepted.

Grenville and his men found Roanoke deserted when they finally returned. Grenville left a few of his crew behind to protect England's claims to Virginia and sailed back to England. The next year, 150 colonists left England to reestablish

Richard Grenville and his fleet returned to Roanoke after the colonists had departed for England.

Roanoke

More than four centuries after its people vanished, the fate of the Roanoke colony remains a mystery. Some investigators believe that Native Americans massacred the colonists. Others believe that colonists intermarried with Native people to secure enough food and improve the odds of survival. Climate scientists have determined that the area suffered a long **drought** before the colony could be resupplied.

a permanent base on Roanoke Island. Grenville's men were nowhere to be found. Expedition leader John White returned to England to request help for the desperate settlement. He brought some of the colonists with him, leaving 115 behind. When he returned three years later, in August 1590, Roanoke was deserted. White could find no trace of the settlement's people.

The Jamestown Colony

By 1606, King James I of England had established the Virginia Company of London to colonize the Chesapeake Bay area, a region surrounded by present-day Maryland and Virginia. In December of that year, Bartholomew Gosnold set sail with dozens of colonists. They sighted land in April 1607 and sailed 50 miles (80 kilometers) inland on the James River. They eventually settled on a marshy peninsula and named their settlement Jamestown.

The Jamestown colonists worked hard to gather resources and build their settlement.

Gosnold and his crew faced severe challenges. There were frequent food shortages. Tensions between colonists and the local Powhatan sometimes erupted in violence. Jamestown's water supply was very salty and unsafe to drink. Tensions also ran high among the colonists. Adventurers fought among themselves, and colonists did not find the gold they desperately sought.

Jamestown was unprofitable and riddled with disease and starvation. The colony soon also found itself at war with the Powhatan. But Jamestown began to thrive as colonists established townships farther inland and

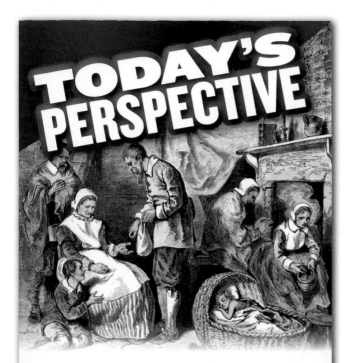

Archaeologists studying the challenges the Jamestown settlers faced once believed that the disease malaria and the constant threat of violence from Native Americans were the main causes of death in the colony. It is now thought that the high content of salt in the drinking water may have caused more deaths than was previously acknowledged. Water evaporation during the hot summers would have further increased the amount of salt in the drinking water to deadly levels.

supply missions became more regular. The introduction of a new type of tobacco gave the colony a profitable export.

New England

In 1607, the British also established Popham colony on the Kennebec River in present-day Maine. The settlers faced food shortages and poor relations with the local Abenaki tribe. The colony collapsed after one year. This caused some explorers to lose interest in coastal New England. Then in 1614, Captain John Smith of Jamestown visited the region and wrote positively about it. His enthusiasm interested a group of English Protestants who sought religious freedom.

In September 1620, 120 hopeful Protestant Pilgrims sailed from Southampton, England, aboard two ships, the *Mayflower* and the *Speedwell*. The smaller *Speedwell* began to take on water and had to abandon the voyage. Continuing alone, the *Mayflower* sighted land at Cape Cod in present-day Massachusetts, near Plymouth Harbor, on November 9. The Virginia Company of London had granted them land farther south near the Hudson River. But with winter quickly approaching, the Pilgrims knew they could not safely continue to their intended destination. They decided to settle near Cape Cod, instead. Before going ashore, the settlers drew up an agreement called the Mayflower Compact. This document established rules for the colony.

The Pilgrims came to North America in search of a home where they could practice their religion freely.

The Pilgrims found cleared fields and a recently abandoned Wampanoag village. They met with little resistance from Native Americans. Still, nearly half the settlers died during the first winter. A Wampanoag named Squanto helped the colonists prepare for their first spring in America by showing them how to grow corn, beans, and squash. He also introduced them to the local Wampanoag chief, Massasoit.

Massasoit was frequently at war with the neighboring Massachusetts and Narragansett tribes, and was eager to sign a treaty with the settlers. He soon tricked the settlers into attacking the Massachusetts tribe. This created tensions between the colonists and the Wampanoag.

The Wampanoag had hoped to develop alliances with the colonists built on trade and shared interests. The Native Americans instead found themselves being treated as inferiors and even intruders. English settlers signed deeds with them, hoping to stake a legal claim to lands. The Native Americans, having no understanding of

A FIRSTHAND LOOK AT
THE MAYFLOWER COMPACT

The Virginia Company of London had originally granted land at the mouth of the Hudson River to the Pilgrims. Instead of proceeding southward, the Pilgrims decided to stay in Plymouth. Because the terms of the charter only applied to the "Virginia territory," the Pilgrims agreed on rules for the new Massachusetts Colony. See page 60 for a link to view a copy of the Mayflower Compact.

The Pilgrims faced many hardships in the early days of Plymouth.

private land ownership, did not realize what changes the English were going to make to their lands. The settlers' steel axes quickly cleared forestlands. Traditional hunting grounds rapidly disappeared.

Most Pilgrims supported themselves by farming, but their fields were small and showed little profit. The colonists had hoped to fish and trade furs to repay the **debts** they ran up for supplies and transportation. The English merchants who financially supported the colony grew impatient because the colony was not making much money. By 1630, Plymouth had a worsening relationship with the Wampanoag and a failing economy. British hopes for establishing successful colonies in America looked bleak.

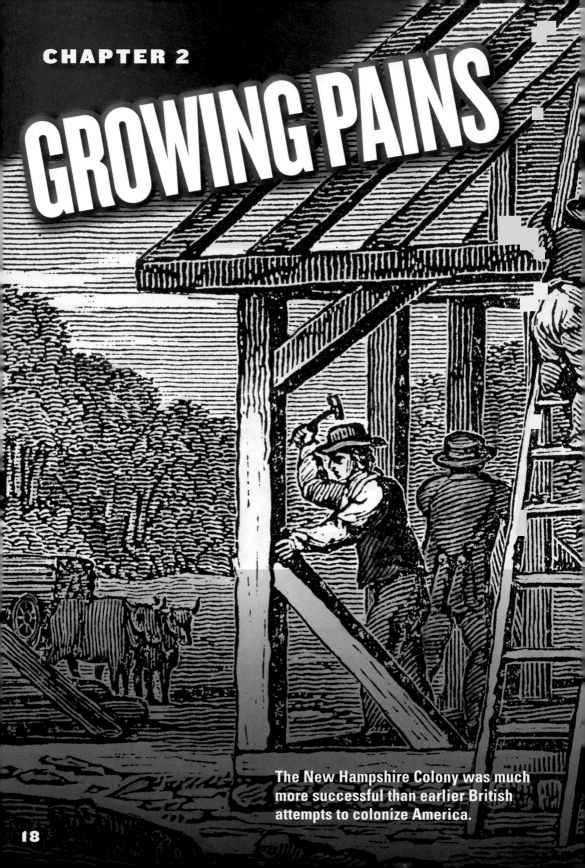

GROWING PAINS

The New Hampshire Colony was much
more successful than earlier British
attempts to colonize America.

AFTER EARLY FAILURES, BRITISH colonization of America began to experience greater success. One of the earliest successful settlements was the New Hampshire Colony. It was established in 1623 by settlers hoping to profit from fishing along the shores of the Great Bay and the Piscataqua River, in present-day New Hampshire and Maine.

Puritan settlers wore simple, traditional clothing.

The Massachusetts Bay Colony

From about 1628 to 1640, roughly 20,000 Puritans made the journey across the Atlantic to settle in New England around the present-day cities of Salem and Boston, Massachusetts. There they established the Massachusetts Bay Colony. The colony was an economic success. It had a thriving trade in shipbuilding, fur, lumber, and fish. The settlers of the Massachusetts Bay Colony also strongly shared their Puritan faith. They believed that members of their community were tied to one another and to God.

Those who would not follow along with these beliefs were asked to leave the colony. When minister Roger Williams repeatedly spoke in favor of religious freedom and separation of church and state, he was summoned before Governor John Winthrop. Williams refused to swear an Oath of Allegiance and Fidelity to the colony, and was sent away from the community. In 1636, Williams and a dozen friends founded a new colony, Providence, in what is now Rhode Island. That same year, Puritan minister Thomas Hooker and 100 followers founded the Connecticut Colony at Hartford.

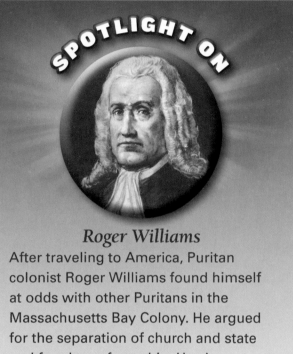

SPOTLIGHT ON

Roger Williams

After traveling to America, Puritan colonist Roger Williams found himself at odds with other Puritans in the Massachusetts Bay Colony. He argued for the separation of church and state and freedom of worship. He also refused to recognize the right of Puritan judges to punish colonists for following other religions. Williams moved to the Plymouth Colony but was disappointed by the church there as well. He returned to Massachusetts, where he was found to be guilty of spreading "dangerous opinions." He was forced out of the colony in 1636.

Taming the Chesapeake Bay

Between 1642 and 1675, another wave of colonists migrated to the Chesapeake Bay area. More than three-quarters of them were **indentured servants**. Merchants paid their passage to the area. The rights to their labor were then sold to tobacco planters, for whom the servants would work for four to seven years. Planters provided the workers with food, clothing, and shelter.

Tobacco planters sold most of their crops to people in Europe.

Some tobacco planters grew wealthy and lived very comfortably.

Growing tobacco in the Chesapeake Bay area became highly profitable for wealthy planters. Small farmers, however, had a hard life. They worked long hours and lived in shabby housing, and within 20 years, their chance for success had vanished. The amount of tobacco that the larger planters were exporting was more than the Europeans could consume. Because the tobacco supply was greater than the demand for it, there was no market for the smaller farmers to sell their product.

The situation was made even worse by Britain's Navigation Acts. These acts required that Chesapeake tobacco be shipped exclusively to England in English

Quaker settlers made a peace agreement with the local Native Americans.

ships. Growers' profits fell sharply. At the same time, expenses of colonial government, including large salaries for Virginia's government leaders, were placed on the shoulders of common planters.

Colonization Surges On

Despite the hardships colonists experienced, people continued to flow into America from Europe. By the early 18th century, emigrants from England, Scotland, and Ireland began pouring into the Delaware River valley. The **Quakers**, already established there, encouraged them to settle in the Appalachian backcountry. There, families worked side by side to clear forests and plant crops.

In addition to new arrivals from overseas, American settlers fanned out from colonies in Massachusetts, the Delaware Valley, and the Chesapeake Bay area to gradually establish colonies from Maine to Georgia. In 1681, Quaker William Penn received a vast piece of land in America from King Charles II. At the same time, Anglicans were making life uncomfortable for Quakers. Quakers were routinely jailed and had their lands seized. Penn established the colony of Pennsylvania. Pennsylvania became a haven for Quakers. It promised colonists freedom of religion, free elections, and trial by jury.

The Pennsylvania Colony was named after founder William Penn.

In 1634, Lord Baltimore of England established the colony of Maryland as a home for English Catholics. Settlements grew up along rivers. Tobacco was the colony's cash crop. In 1732, James Oglethorpe established the colony of Georgia.

The establishment of Georgia increased the number of British colonies in America to 13. In order of their founding, they were: Virginia (1607), Massachusetts (1620), New Hampshire (1623), Maryland (1634), Connecticut (1636), Rhode Island (1636), Delaware (1638), North Carolina (1653), South Carolina (1663), New Jersey (1664), New York (1664), Pennsylvania (1682), and Georgia (1732).

Catholic settlers held services and constructed churches in the Maryland Colony.

Colonists brutally murdered most of the residents of a Pequot village in May 1637.

A Clash of Cultures

Colonial relations with Native Americans often resulted in conflict. Frequent battles, raids, and wars by both sides usually resulted in Native American defeat and loss of land. The constant warfare and deadly diseases that settlers had brought with them from Europe also killed many native people.

In 1636, British colonists met stiff resistance from the Pequot in Connecticut's Mystic River valley. When a trader was killed, colonists blamed the Pequot. The Massachusetts and Connecticut colonies promptly declared war on them. The Mohegan and Narragansett were enemies of the Pequot. They sided with the colonists. In May 1637, colonists surrounded a Pequot village and set it ablaze. The killing continued until almost

YESTERDAY'S HEADLINES

Writing from England, Reverend John Robinson (above, center) scolded the Plymouth Colony for "the killing of those poor Indians," adding, "How happy a thing it had been, if you had converted some before you had killed any." Puritan leaders responded, establishing several new praying towns. These settlements forced Native Americans to adopt English dress and the Puritan religion. Many colonists distrusted them. They continued to think of the Native Americans as "savages."

all of the Pequot were dead or sold to the Narragansett.

By the late 1640s, Puritan missionaries began encouraging Native Americans to live in permanent communities. In these "praying towns," the Native Americans were encouraged to adopt English dress and agricultural techniques, and to embrace Puritanism. Praying-town Native Americans sometimes acted as colonial informants and were disliked by other Native Americans. Three Wampanoag killed one such informant in 1675. Plymouth colonists retaliated by hanging the three men. Led by Chief Metacom, also called King Philip, Wampanoag warriors burned colonial homesteads in response.

On the Virginia frontiers, the Susquehannock raided farms and killed settlers. However, Governor

Colonial attempts to convert Native Americans to Puritan ways led to the violence of King Philip's War.

William Berkeley insisted that the settlers not seek revenge because he did not want to risk the profitable deerskin trade with the Susquehannock. In 1676, Virginia colonist Nathaniel Bacon defied these government orders and led 1,000 Virginians in a bloody uprising against the Native Americans. Bacon's Rebellion briefly drove Berkeley from power.

Farther north, a Wampanoag uprising, called King Philip's War (1675–1676), soon grew to include the powerful Narragansett and other tribes. Native

Americans attacked more than half of the region's 90 Puritan towns. The colonists responded by building alliances with the Mohegan and Pequot. Eventually, the tide of battle turned. The Narragansett ran out of food and ammunition, and the rebellion collapsed.

The Clouds of War

By 1760, the population of British America had grown to about two million people. To meet their needs, land companies looked westward toward the Ohio River valley for trade and settlement opportunities. The French, believing their fur trade with Native Americans in the Ohio Valley would be threatened, attacked and destroyed British trading outposts.

French settlers established a profitable fur trade with local Native Americans.

The French and Indian War marked a major turning point in the relationship between the colonists and the British.

The British government in England was outraged by the French attacks. Trade with their American colonies had become highly profitable. The British would defend their investments even at the risk of war. In a rare act of colonial cooperation, representatives from seven colonies met in Albany, New York, in June 1754 to discuss the situation. Before a plan could be finalized, war broke out in Ohio. Its consequences would change life in the 13 colonies forever.

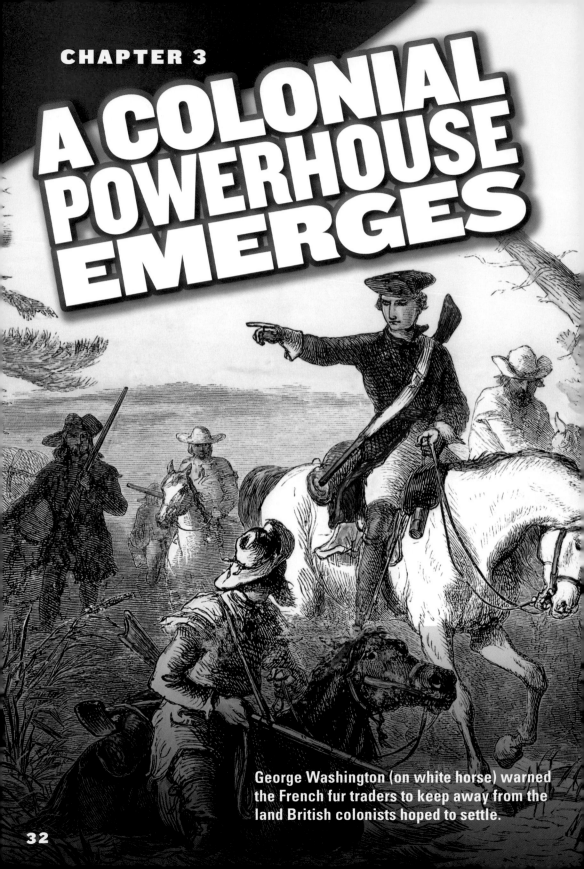

CHAPTER 3

A COLONIAL POWERHOUSE EMERGES

George Washington (on white horse) warned the French fur traders to keep away from the land British colonists hoped to settle.

THE FRENCH AND INDIAN WAR

(1754-1763) began as a series of small frontier battles between the French and British colonists. In 1753, the governor of Virginia had sent a young officer named George Washington to warn the French to advance no farther in Ohio. However, they ignored the warning. Washington's **militia** was sent out to regain the territory when French and Native American forces occupied the region. Instead, Washington was captured. Britain responded by sending troops under British command to work with colonial forces and launch attacks on the French.

A VIEW FROM ABROAD

British general Edward Braddock expected to be warmly received by the American colonists he had come to protect against the French and their native allies during the French and Indian War. However, most colonists were not cooperative. Braddock complained about their "slothful and languid disposition," claiming they were "very unfit for military service." British general James Wolfe added, "The Americans are in general the dirtiest, most contemptible cowardly dogs that you can conceive. There is no depending on them in action."

The Cost of Victory

France's Native American allies repeatedly ambushed outnumbered British troops along the colonial frontiers. Delaware and Shawnee tribes launched assaults on Virginia and Pennsylvania. But the war eventually began to turn in Britain's favor in 1757, when William Pitt was named British secretary of state. Pitt sharply increased British military support for the colonies and expanded colonial militias.

The 1763 signing of the Treaty of Paris ended the war. Britain was victorious. The treaty made it the dominant European power in America. Within months of the treaty's signing, Britain's king George III issued a proclamation reserving lands west of the Appalachian Mountains for Native Americans. The Proclamation of 1763 was unpopular with colonists, who wanted those territories for themselves.

The Proclamation of 1763 limited colonists to the region east of the Appalachian Mountains. British leaders hoped this would stop conflicts between Native Americans and the colonists. However, many colonists had purchased or had been given land west of the Appalachians for their military service during the French and Indian War. The proclamation was one of the milestones in the rising tensions between Great Britain and the colonies. See page 60 for a link to view the original proclamation online.

Tobacco and the Plantation System

By the mid-18th century, tobacco was the main export of British America. In 1700, 28 million pounds of tobacco were exported. The amount had nearly tripled sixty

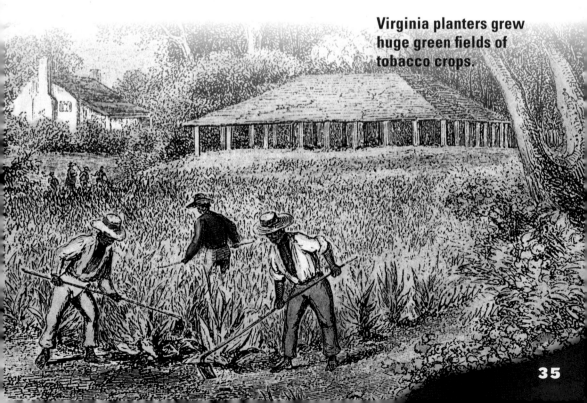

Virginia planters grew huge green fields of tobacco crops.

years later. Virginia was the primary grower and exporter of tobacco. The largest amounts of tobacco were grown on huge plantations.

The plantation system required large numbers of laborers. At first, indentured servants were the main source of workers. Then African slaves were brought to America to take the place of indentured servants.

Planters were often frustrated by slaves' efforts to run away or avoid the plantation's endless work. Many planters whipped and beat their slaves. This

Slaves were forced to spend long hours working grueling jobs.

Because slaves were considered personal property, owners could buy and sell them as they saw fit.

only increased slave resistance. Planters sought other solutions for running their plantations. In 1718, Great Britain passed a law allowing the transport of convicts to America. By 1760, 20,000 convicts had been sent to the Chesapeake Bay area. They supplemented slave labor and indentured servitude.

Even Less Freedom

Throughout these early years in America, more and more laws were put in place regarding slavery. Beginning

YESTERDAY'S HEADLINES

The 1739 Stono Rebellion fueled the worst fears of South Carolina planters. Led by a slave named Jemmy, the 20 escaped slaves had once been soldiers in Africa. They stole guns and went on a killing spree. They recruited dozens more slaves and burned seven plantations to the ground before the rebellion was put down violently by the South Carolina militia. The following year, the colony passed laws that prohibited slaves from earning money, learning to read, and gathering in groups.

in 1650, Virginia, Maryland, and South Carolina passed a series of slave codes to restrict the movement and freedom of African slaves. In 1662, Virginia declared that the children of enslaved mothers were also slaves. In 1705, a new code stated that slaves were considered personal property. The same law protected planters from punishment if they killed slaves while whipping them.

Some planters feared slaves. They believed the slaves would eventually rebel against their owners. These fears became reality on September 9, 1739, near Charleston, South Carolina. Twenty runaway slaves seized weapons and ammunition from a store at Stono River Bridge. They burned several plantations and killed around 25 white people.

That same year, a law in South Carolina forbade freeing slaves or concealing runaways. That law also established fines and jail terms for anyone who taught slaves to read and write.

The Economies of Northern and Southern Colonies

Agriculture provided the economic basis of the southern colonies, although half of the white farmers did not own

Wheat was a common crop in some colonies.

slaves and were not involved in tobacco export. Instead, they grew corn and wheat. They also kept cattle and hogs.

Northern colonies had a more diverse economy. Mid-Atlantic farmers sometimes had indentured servants, but they were uncommon farther north in New England. Most farms there were small. Many grew corn, wheat, barley, or rye. The farmers raised cattle, hogs, and chickens. Because northern crops required less labor than tobacco, the northern colonies had less need for slaves than the southern colonies did.

Some colonial farmers kept chickens and other livestock.

Slavery enabled colonial planters to thrive by providing an inexpensive source of labor.

However, slavery was legal in all of the northern colonies. As early as 1641, Massachusetts provided the first official recognition of slavery in British North America. Within a few years, Plymouth, Connecticut, Rhode Island, New York, and New Jersey passed similar laws, establishing legal slavery years before it was established in the South.

By 1760, Britain's 13 American colonies had become an economic powerhouse. Trade among colonies grew. Colonial exports became steadily more profitable. A new era of prosperity was dawning. This prosperity also brought new challenges.

CHAPTER 4
THE COMING STORM

By the mid-1700s, American cities such as New York had become bustling economic centers.

AS LONG AS THE AMERICAN
colonies continued to supply England with
produce and manufactured goods, the mother
country saw no need to place heavy taxes upon
them. But the French and Indian War had been
extremely expensive. Britain had accumulated
considerable debt protecting its colonial interests
and the lives of its subjects, the American
colonists. It therefore looked to the colonies as the
source of money it needed to pay off its debt.

Taxation Without Representation

In 1761, Boston lawyer James Otis, who represented Britain's interests in the city's Admiralty Court, announced that he would resign his position rather than serve search warrants used to collect taxes. Otis believed that if Americans were going to be taxed, they should have representatives in Parliament, the British lawmaking body. His phrase "Taxation without representation is tyranny" became a rallying cry for dissatisfied American colonists.

British prime minister George Grenville's taxes made him extremely unpopular among the American colonists.

In 1764, Britain's prime minister George Grenville created new taxes. The Sugar Act placed heavy taxes on sugar, coffee, textiles, and silk imported from other countries. The Currency Act banned the creation and use of paper money in the colonies. At a meeting in Boston, unhappy colonists signed a pledge to **boycott** many British imports. Within a few months, several colonies signed the Non-Importation Agreement. This stated that merchants and traders would not import items from or export items to Britain.

TODAY'S PERSPECTIVE

Many historians believe that the French and Indian War was the fault of the American colonists. The French realized that the Ohio region was ideal for fur trading, so they claimed it as their own. Then the colony of Virginia claimed it as well. Neither France nor Britain cared enough to fight over the territory until Virginian colonists swarmed in to grab land and interfere with France's fur trade. When French troops were sent on a peace mission into an area occupied by the colonists, a colonial militia fired on them. Britain was then dragged into a full-blown conflict to protect the American colonists.

Parliament ignored the storm brewing in the colonies. It approved the Stamp Act in March 1765. A royal

The Stamp Act of 1765 required that colonists pay a tax on every piece of printed paper they used. Legal documents, licenses, newspapers, and even playing cards were taxed. The Stamp Act caused an outcry heard throughout the colonies and fueled American anger toward Britain. See page 60 for a link to view the contents of the Stamp Act online.

stamp had to be purchased and attached to every legal document and newspaper. Americans were further angered because the money raised by the tax paid for unwanted British soldiers who remained behind after the French and Indian War. Making matters worse, the newly structured courts could try violators of the Stamp Act.

The colonists were outraged when they received news of the Stamp Act.

Some colonists protested the Stamp Act by burning stamps and other paper goods.

The Colonists Respond

In Boston, Samuel Adams organized a group called the Sons of Liberty to terrorize royal stamp agents. Similar groups sprang up across New England. The same year, Parliament approved the Mutiny Act. It required colonists to **quarter** British troops. Colonial lawmakers responded by refusing to fund the quartering of troops.

Resistance to Grenville's laws quickly spread. Speaking before Virginia's colonial legislature in 1765, Patrick Henry introduced seven resolutions, called the Virginia Resolves. The seventh declared Virginia's freedom to

Samuel Adams successfully persuaded colonists to rally against the Stamp Act.

make its own laws. In October of that year, delegates from nine colonies met in a Stamp Act Congress in New York City and published a 14-point Declaration of Rights and Grievances. The declaration denied the right of Parliament to force taxes on the 13 colonies and establish royal courts. Grenville responded by raising troops to enforce the Stamp Act. Benjamin Franklin persuaded Grenville that such an action would only fan the flames of rebellion. The Stamp Act was ended in March 1766.

Parliament quickly passed the Revenue Act. It placed taxes on imported lead, paper, glass, and tea. The taxes were to be used to pay for royal colonial officials. But royal **customs** commissioners abused the power they had been given. They seized merchant vessels that did not follow the strict rules of the Revenue Act and charged huge fines. If fines went unpaid, they sold the ships and the cargo.

In 1768, Pennsylvanian John Dickinson published *Letters from a Farmer in Pennsylvania to the Inhabitants of the British Colonies*, a collection of letters addressed to his "Beloved Countrymen." *Letters* was published throughout the colonies and in England. By 1770, colonial protests

Benjamin Franklin convinced Parliament that it would be nearly impossible to enforce the Stamp Act.

YESTERDAY'S HEADLINES

John Dickinson's (above) *Letters from a Farmer in Pennsylvania to the Inhabitants of the British Colonies* played a crucial role in the development of what became the American Revolution. Addressed to the common person, the letters discussed the necessary limitations of government. They were widely read throughout the colonies and in Britain. They rallied America and made some members of Parliament more sympathetic to the colonists' concerns. Dickinson's letters informed Europe about the growing rebellion in America and forced Britain to abolish the Revenue Act, leaving only its tax on imported tea.

forced Britain to repeal all of the taxes in the Revenue Act except the unpopular tax on tea. In response, on December 16, 1773, the Sons of Liberty boarded three British ships loaded with crates of tea. They disguised themselves as Mohawks and dumped 342 chests of tea into Boston Harbor. The event became known as the Boston Tea Party.

Britain Fires Back

Angered by the colonists' actions, Parliament approved the Coercive Acts, which closed the port of Boston and made plans to quarter troops permanently in the city. In 1774,

Thomas Gage served as governor of the Massachusetts Colony from 1774 to 1775.

King George III sent General Thomas Gage to Boston, where he would serve as royal governor. Gage ordered the colonists' General Assembly to make Salem the new capital of the colony. Instead, the assembly made plans for all 13 colonies to unite and form the Continental Congress. America's colonies were unable to look back. They marched toward revolution and a future they could scarcely have imagined.

MAP OF THE EVENTS

What Happened Where?

FRENCH
TERRITORY

APPALACHIAN

Proclamation
line of 1763

SC
1788

GA
1788

N
W   E
S

0   150   300 mi

0   150   300 km

SPANISH
TERRITORY

SPANISH
TERR.

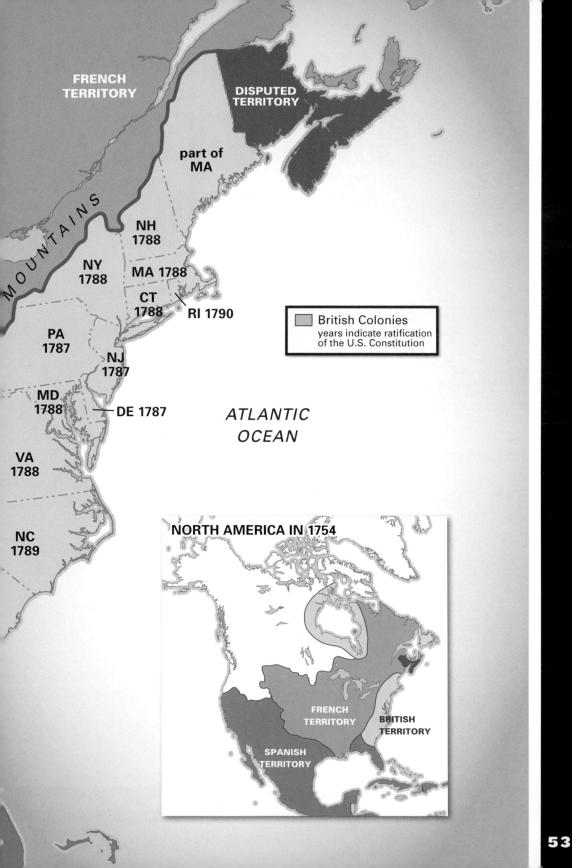

FRENCH
TERRITORY

DISPUTED
TERRITORY

part of
MA

M O U N T A I N S

NH
1788

NY
1788

MA 1788

CT
1788

RI 1790

PA
1787

NJ
1787

MD
1788

DE 1787

VA
1788

NC
1789

British Colonies
years indicate ratification
of the U.S. Constitution

ATLANTIC
OCEAN

NORTH AMERICA IN 1754

FRENCH
TERRITORY

BRITISH
TERRITORY

SPANISH
TERRITORY

A Legacy of Freedom

In 1776, the Declaration of Independence marked the colonies' official separation from British rule.

The greatness of America resides in its legacy of freedom. That freedom did not come easily. It was earned by hard work and suffering—and sometimes at the expense of others' rights and freedoms.

JULY 4 IS THE ANNIVERSARY OF THE ADOPTION

In their humble beginnings, colonial settlements struggled against disease, Native Americans, and even one another. They worked to build economic success in a land of vast resources. Colonists fought for the right to practice religion according to their beliefs. Many planters became wealthy by enslaving people taken from their African homelands and denying them the most basic human rights. Colonists secured the frontiers by stripping Native Americans of their land and heritage, and pushing them ever westward to the margins of a land that had once been their own.

Today, we still struggle with this mixed legacy. The liberty that defines America makes it a beacon to the world. There are still many inequalities to be overcome, but advances have been made and the work continues. America's legacy is still being written.

After the Revolutionary War, George Washington became the first president of the newly formed United States of America.

OF THE DECLARATION OF INDEPENDENCE.

Roger Williams

Bartholomew Gosnold (1572–1607) was an explorer and lawyer who helped found the Virginia Company of London and commanded one of the ships that landed at Jamestown.

John Smith (1580–1631) was a British explorer and one of the leaders of the Jamestown Colony. He built alliances with the Powhatan and his writings created interest in the colonization of America.

John Winthrop (ca. 1587–1649) was a Puritan lawyer and governor of the Massachusetts Bay Colony for 12 of the first 20 years of the colony's existence.

Roger Williams (ca. 1603–1683) was a supporter of religious freedom and separation of church and state. He was banished from the Massachusetts Bay Colony and established the Rhode Island Colony.

William Berkeley (ca. 1605–1677) was governor of the Virginia Colony for almost 30 years. He believed in free trade and opposed religious freedom and public education.

Metacom (King Philip) (ca. 1639–1676) was a Wampanoag chief and leader in King Philip's War (1675–1676), a Native American uprising against English colonists in New England.

William Penn (1644–1718) was a Quaker businessman and philosopher who founded the Pennsylvania Colony and promised democracy, religious freedom, and positive relations with Native Americans.

Nathaniel Bacon (1647–1676) was a settler of the Virginia Colony who led an uprising in 1676 against Governor William Berkeley when Berkeley failed to protect frontier settlers against Native American attacks.

William Penn

Benjamin Franklin (1706–1790) was a statesman, scientist, diplomat, and leading spokesman for American interests in England who negotiated the repeal of the Stamp Act with British prime minister George Grenville in 1766.

George Grenville (1712–1770) was the British prime minister from 1763 to 1765 and the enforcer of the unpopular Revenue Act, Currency Act, and Stamp Act.

George Grenville

Samuel Adams (1722–1803) was an American statesman and founder of Boston's Sons of Liberty. He became one of the leading figures in the American Revolution.

Patrick Henry (1736–1799) was a politician and lawyer who introduced the Virginia Resolves before Virginia's colonial legislature in defiance of the Stamp Act.

TIMELINE

1565
Spain establishes a permanent settlement at St. Augustine.

1584
An English expedition lands in present-day North Carolina.

1590
A resupply mission discovers that Roanoke colony has disappeared.

1637
English settlers wage the Pequot massacre near the Mystic River in Connecticut.

1642–1675
A wave of migration to the Chesapeake Bay area occurs.

1675–1676
King Philip's War is fought.

1754–1763
The French and Indian War is fought.

1763
The Treaty of Paris is signed; the Proclamation of 1763 is issued.

1765
The British encourage the Stamp Act and the Virginia Resolves are issued.

1607

English settlers establish a colony at Jamestown.

1620

The *Mayflower* lands at Plymouth; the Mayflower Compact is drawn up.

1628–1640

A massive emigration from Great Britain to New England occurs; the Massachusetts Bay Colony is founded.

1676

Bacon's Rebellion is waged in the Virginia Colony.

1705

Slave codes make slaves personal property.

1739

The Stono Rebellion is waged by slaves in the colony of South Carolina.

1768

John Dickinson's *Letters from a Farmer in Pennsylvania* is published.

1773

The Boston Tea Party occurs.

1774

The port of Boston is closed by British authorities.

LIVING HISTORY

Primary sources provide firsthand evidence about a topic. Witnesses to a historical event create primary sources. They include autobiographies, newspaper reports of the time, oral histories, photographs, and memoirs. A secondary source analyzes primary sources, and is one step or more removed from the event. Secondary sources include textbooks, encyclopedias, and commentaries. To view the following primary and secondary sources, go to www.factsfornow.scholastic.com. Enter the keywords **British Colonies** and look for the Living History logo Σ¦.

Σ¦ **The Mayflower Compact** In 1620, Pilgrim colonists signed an agreement on how they would govern their colony before stepping off the *Mayflower* at Plymouth, Massachusetts. You can view a copy of the original document online.

Σ¦ **The Oath of Allegiance and Fidelity** Colonists in Massachusetts Bay had to promise not to oppose the will of the colony or act to overthrow it. You can view the text of the oath online.

Σ¦ **The Proclamation of 1763** The Proclamation of 1763 was issued following the French and Indian War. It limited colonists to the land east of the Appalachian Mountains. You can view the original document online.

Σ¦ **The Stamp Act** The Stamp Act required colonists to pay a tax on all printed paper. It was protested widely and served as a major motivation toward the growing resistance to British rule. You can read the text of the act online.

RESOURCES

Books

Benoit, Peter. *The Jamestown Colony.* Danbury, CT: Children's Press, 2012.

Cunningham, Kevin. *The Boston Tea Party.* Danbury, CT: Children's Press, 2012.

Gregory, Josh. *The Revolutionary War.* Danbury, CT: Children's Press, 2012.

Hakim, Joy. *Making Thirteen Colonies: 1600–1740.* New York: Oxford University Press, 2007.

Richards, Elizabeth. *The Founding of a Nation.* Mustang, OK: Tate Publishing, 2008.

Visit this Scholastic Web site for more information on the British Colonies: www.factsfornow.scholastic.com Enter the keywords British Colonies

GLOSSARY

boycott (BOI-kaht) a refusal to buy goods from a person, group, or country

customs (KUHS-tumz) duties or taxes placed on goods imported from another country

debts (DETZ) money or other things that people owe

drought (DROUT) a long period without rain

economic (eh-kuh-NAH-mik) relating to the system of producing, distributing, and consuming goods and services

indentured servants (in-DEN-shurd SUR-vuhnts) workers bound to work for a certain period of time in exchange for food, housing, transport from overseas, and land

militia (muh-LISH-uh) a group of people who are trained to fight but who are not professional soldiers

privateer (prye-vuh-TEER) an individual or a ship who is hired to attack enemy ships during wartime but is not a part of the military

Quakers (KWAY-kurz) members of the Society of Friends, a Christian group that prefers simple religious services and opposes war

quarter (KWOR-tur) to provide soldiers with food and a place to sleep

INDEX

Page numbers in *italics* indicate illustrations.

ABOUT THE AUTHOR

Peter Benoit is a graduate of Skidmore College in Saratoga Springs, New York. His degree is in mathematics. He is the author of dozens of books with Children's Press and has written on topics as diverse as Native Americans, ecosystems, disasters, American history, and ancient civilizations. Peter has also written more than 2,000 poems. He lives in Greenwich, New York.